MAN OF SORROWS

by

Kelli Rae Hurst

Dedication

This book is dedicated to all who wonder.
This book is dedicated to any who believe there is more.
This book is dedicated to those who ask questions.
This book is dedicated to hearts who long to explore.

This book is dedicated to a People with pain.
This book is dedicated to ones surrounded by closed doors.
This book is dedicated to beings who hunger.
This book is dedicated to the souls whom He adores.

Our eyes wider open;
Our ears fully attune.
May truth rise beloved.
May we behold the beauty that is You.

Acknowledgements

Special thanks to my exceptional and endearing husband, Vincent.
Your wisdom is golden; your steadfastness, inspiring.

Special thanks to my sister-friend, Megan.
Your encouragement and support are not of this world.

Special thanks to my favorites, Gregg and Polly.
Your simultaneous honesty and acceptance are a breath of holy air.

Special thanks to the Ones, without whom, there would be nothing—
Father. Son. Holy Spirit.

Foreword

This is a beautiful work inspired by the greatest story ever told—simply, the Gospel. There is an elegant application of paternal love, commitment, and devotion. One of the most interesting aspects of Kelli's perspective is the uncompromising truth of God's word.

We sometimes miss truth, not despite its obviousness, but because of it. It's just too good to be true!

As a student of God's word, I applaud the subtle way this book unfolds and illuminates the curiosity of the reader. Her work is fascinating and provocative. Kelli has the ability to look at mundane facts and extract the deep treasure that lies within. It guides us through the humble beginning, the excruciating conflict, the rejection, the trial, and the predictable end. And then, with perfect clarity, we are privy to the greatest plot twist of all time; here, our Champion, Redeemer, and King, enters in to his glory!

The ages old question is then answered…. "Why?".

-Pastor Matt Morgan
Fellowship of Praise Church, Clarksville, Ohio

"Like a young plant or a root
that sprouts in dry ground,
the servant grew up
obeying the Lord.
He wasn't some handsome king.
Nothing about the way he looked
made him attractive to us.
He was hated and rejected;
his life was filled with sorrow
and terrible suffering.
No one wanted to look at him.
We despised him and said,
"He is a nobody!"
He suffered and endured
great pain for us...
He was wounded and crushed
because of our sins...

All of us were like sheep
that had wandered off.
We had each gone our own way,
but the Lord gave him
the punishment we deserved.
He was painfully abused,
but he did not complain...
He was condemned to death
without a fair trial.
Who could have imagined
what would happen to him?...
He wasn't dishonest or violent,
but he was buried in a tomb
of cruel and rich people...
Others thought he was a sinner,
but he suffered for our sins
and asked God to forgive us."

-Isaiah 53:2-12 CEV
The Bible

Elohim, the great and immeasurable God who saw all, made all, knew all, and tended all, lived in Paradise. He was purely good and thoroughly just. He was, in image and expression, love. He was made of brilliant light, and sat upon a blazing, immovable throne crowning all things ever in existence, shrouded in prismatic color and showered in unending song.

He had a single, cherished Son. Elohim and the Son's love for each other and for all things was a powerful energy that permeated every particle of every realm. It reverberated throughout all time and space. It was paradise in Paradise.

Outside of Paradise, was a different story.

The People were the beings Elohim had created for his Son as an expression of his great love. Like a bride for a groom, they were a very special gift for his very special Son. They were so special, they were the only creation he ever made with a similarity to himself. He and the Son, with great attention, carefully crafted a special planet and a Place of Pleasures that mirrored their own Paradise for them to dwell in. They even gave them a measure of their own great power and authority to rule in that realm. But, the People made a mess of it...

again... and again... and again... and again...

and again.

Elohim loved the People as much as his own Son. He didn't understand why they would want anything other than the breathtaking one he had made them for—the Son. The Son was the darling of Paradise; God himself. Anything one would admire or desire, he was it. All creatures adored him; wanted to be near him; were drawn to him like flowers to the sun. His presence was the purest euphoria. Why didn't the People appreciate what, and who, Elohim had given to them? He was perfect in wisdom and character. How could he relate to a people who had become so disloyal and unreasonable?

Elohim once enjoyed endless togetherness with the People. The first breath they took was the one he breathed into them. But, they eventually turned aside from Elohim's protective path, and simultaneously allowed the devastating and polluting effects of Hades, and it's offspring, Confusion, into their once utopian home. Because of his nature being the very substance of justice, Elohim could no longer remain there with them. Their togetherness had been broken.

Although they had hurt him, Elohim was zealous for them and wanted them back. He wasn't going to give up on what he treasured most so easily. He was unmatched in his ability to fix things and make them beautiful again, in restoring things that had been lost. Out of this came his plan for the People.

Elohim would send the Son to them.

The Condescent

The Son would come to the People differently than he ever had before. His Spirit had been with them at times. He had also come in veiled versions of his glorious, gleaming self. This time, however, he would make himself as one of them. Feel what they feel. Experience what they experience. Hurt how they hurt. In *every* way. Through this, he would rebuild what they had torn down, and retrieve what they had lost—togetherness with the One who made them. Togetherness with him was *everything*, for through him, everything came.

They were his. Now, through the Son, he was going to make himself theirs.

Forever this time.

The Rising Sun dawned; the Son entered his creation.

It was not a grand, dazzling entrance one would expect for The King. When he arrived, he was welcomed by the stench of dirt, animals, and manure; without ritual, fanfare, or dignity.

He did not come as a grown person, able to do everything for Himself. He came the same way all the People did—as a tiny seed. He had to grow slowly, day by day, hidden and reliant on the attention and protection of his mother carrying him. Once The All-Powerful; now weak, helpless, and utterly dependent on others to meet his needs and take care of him.

Like the People, he grew having to learn everything from nothing: how to survive in the world, how to contribute to his family, even how to take orders and obey. He also had to learn what it meant to not be able to do many things that he saw others doing. He had to learn not to compare his life with others'; to embrace his own design and destiny. He was meant for more than what he experienced in the day-to-day. But often, that felt like a very lonely place.

No Stranger to Weakness

The Son was not born into privilege. He was born into a poor, lower-class family, in a town that was considered good-for-nothing, and at a time without modern convenience or benefits.

Royalty had become peasantry. The Ruler of Galaxies was now subject to great disadvantage, restriction, and constraint; subject to these People he had made from dirt.

Formerly secure——now vulnerable.

3

Not only did the Son choose to leave his supernatural realm and enter the realm of natural law, shadow, and poverty, but he was also born a refugee. In the Son's early days, the leader of the People was a power-hungry murderer who was exterminating large numbers of his own kind, children specifically, of which, the Son was targeted. The Son's family had to flee their home, and all that was familiar, for sanctuary in a foreign country. The Son learned what it meant to be displaced and live in danger, insecurity, uncertainty, and unrest. He was beginning to get to know this world of war, chaos, and confusion.

But the Son faced another issue early in his life with the People.

Although he was once crowned with greatest honor, on this planet he was born in a manner that was questionable, at best, to those who knew of his family. It was apparent that his mother had conceived while only engaged to the man that would ultimately raise him, Joseph. Although she was pure when she became pregnant with the Son, who would have believed it? It was the utmost of disgraces, one that would have labeled them disreputable and dishonorable, placing great stigma upon them. The Son, no doubt, had all manner of lies and gossip spread about him throughout his formative years because of his assumed origin. He likely wrestled with feelings of illegitimacy, being misunderstood and devalued, and certainly, not fitting in.

He was The Treasure of Greatest Value, but now had become an outcast.

Judging The Judge

As the Son grew older, he became well-acquainted with unfair government systems, oppression, racism, insults, and being taken advantage of. He was born a Jew, a race despised by all including the Romans who ruled over them. On a whim, they would force the Jews to do work for them. They often treated them with cruelty and brutality, leaving them defenseless, with no one to represent them. In fact, the Son would have been very well acquainted with the many Roman forms of punishment, including the gruesome, drawn-out process of execution called crucifixion. They saved crucifixion for the most despised criminals, for it was the worst thing they could conceive to do to a person. There was even a time when the Romans lined the roads to the city for miles with crucified Jews, hanging on crosses as symbols of their iron grip on them.

The Son's hometown was a wrong-side-of-the-tracks sort of place. His district, by outsiders including other Jews, was considered fitting for only undignified simpletons and rebels. Making it impossible to conceal their native roots, they had an accent that gave them away immediately. It was bad enough to have to deal with Jews at all, but this stretch of land was the last place a Roman soldier would want to be stationed.

The Future That Awaits

The Jews lived their lives under a weighty umbrella of foreign hostility. Because of the Roman's expressed irritation and general poor treatment of them, they longed for a change. The People worked in fragile tension, never knowing what each day might bring. Their days eked by in anxious and laborious waiting; waiting for a Rescuer——a unique individual specifically sent by Elohim who, they hoped, would liberate them. But there had long since been any hint of his coming. Hopes thinned.

The Son now found himself to be an interwoven part of the lowest, most marginalized and persecuted People ever in history.

He had come to lighten loads, but in this realm, he was merely a burden.

The Son inhabited a very dark and obscure time in history. Ages, centuries even, had passed since the People had someone to tell them what Elohim was saying. It had been like an enduring drought in their spirits. Their lack of connection to the one who made them, Elohim, was taking its inevitable toll. The inner longing for more, to be anchored to something steadfast instead of being blown around aimlessly by the dark and unpredictable winds of life was palpable. Civilization reflected this in the way the People treated each other: envy, animosity, cheating, prejudices... You could feel the desperation in the air.

During this time, however, a splinter of light began to shine through the encompassing curtain of endless night. There was a man named John who was the Son's cousin by birth. He broke the drought. He told the People they needed to turn from their way of doing things, and turn back toward Elohim's way. John foretold that a Rescuer would soon be coming. A Rescuer he believed would save the People from Hades and Confusion. This was Elohim's plan, and the People needed to get ready for this Rescuer's coming. Feelings of hope and wonder began to sprout. Could the change they've been waiting for really be near? Would they dare to believe?

Not only did John help prepare the People to receive the Son——their Rescuer——when he stepped out onto the public scene shortly thereafter, but the Son loved John very much. John was the best man the Son knew. He paved the way for the Son's place in the hearts of the People. To the Son, John was special; a man of unique worth. Tragically, like so many things in that realm riddled with voids and vacuums, this irreplaceable friend would be prematurely taken away from him.

The Son was a vast, overflowing spring of affection and devotion. He was always watering souls. And receiving so little in return.

The one thing that helped the Son overcome the difficulties of this life was that he spent much of his time alone, conversing with his Father, Elohim. The Son drew strength, understanding, and ability from the supernatural realm into the natural realm through this loving, reciprocated connection. This connection was the channel through which the two realms intertwined. Elohim longed to have this same connection and relationship with the People—the very reason he relinquished his prized Son in the first place. And now the Son was getting a clearer picture day by day of his Father's plan. And the time for that plan's fulfillment was drawing near.

So, the Son was compelled to go out into the wild.

He needed to prepare himself for what Elohim sent him to do. He needed to remove himself from certain things; normal daily activity, distraction, even basic needs like food and shelter. He was hungry. He was weak. He was isolated. He chose to forego the comforts People often cling to. He emptied himself entirely so that he could be filled with more of who Elohim was; his presence, his Spirit, his essence—his words, guidance, comfort and reassurance. He knew he needed him, and would need him in increasing measure, for things to come.

The Son was the only one who could truly do whatever he desired, and yet, was openly embracing the position of doing nothing he desired.

So, for forty days he went without. He had desires and temptations for the things he had put aside, and more. He was tempted in the same ways the People were: to choose what feels good over what is right; to look out for personal well-being over the well-being of others; to sacrifice the long-term for the immediate. These temptations did not stop there. After later leaving his home, he lived as a nomad and vagabond. He was in a position of having to rely on the benevolence of others to provide for his everyday needs. He had nothing. He could have had everything, and not so long ago did. But he instead took on the role of a servant. He had deity flowing through his veins, and still The Most Important One chose to view himself as less important. So, he was glad to spend his time with the rejects, misfits, outcasts, criminals, disabled, diseased, homeless, and sinful——those that society considered unworthy or irredeemable.

The Son had access to everything one would need or desire; but he gave it all away, keeping nothing back for himself.

Following several years of this lifestyle, the apex of the Son's intent to permanently mend the People's severed relationship with Elohim was achingly close.

He had been through waiting. He had been through preparation. He had been, and still was, going through the process. In his short life with the People, he had experienced loss, grief, sadness, and a broken heart. His beloved friend and cousin John had been murdered. The man who raised him as a father had likely died also. He had, at one point, lost another very close friend named Lazarus.

But he was experiencing very different feelings now.

As he knelt in a shadowy garden, in a grim and miserable state, he was aware that an angry mob of the People was on its way to deliver him to the same extreme suffering he had seen inflicted on unfortunate others at the hands of the Romans.

The feelings of dread, anxiety, sorrow, hopelessness, and powerlessness overwhelmed him to the point he was sweating blood. The feelings so intense, so terrible, he felt he could die right there.

Nonetheless, he woefully bowed his will to Elohim's will. Despite the emotional and mental storm that was brewing all around him, he chose to move forward with this plan. He could have called off the whole thing. But what of the People? He would lose them...again. No——he had to persevere.

Gethsemane: Garden of Pressing

Amid his despair, his very closest friends——those that said they believed who he said he was, those who were practically family, those who had been with him since the beginning of his vagrancy—— didn't understand at all what he was going through. Despite all that they had seen and heard in their time with him, that their Rescuer would knowingly hand over his life and die was too unbelievable still. So, for the Son, there was no one to commiserate with. He had no one giving him sympathy. He had tried to explain to them the great horrors he was about to go through, but they didn't get it.

He was on his own.

8

There were others at play in this story——the Religion leaders. They were greatly offended by the Son. They didn't like the things he did. They didn't like the things he said. They looked down on the People who followed him, and most of all, they didn't like how he uncovered the false things they were doing. They were the Jews with power, and the Son exposed how they were leading the People away from truth and into lies. They had been doing things this way for hundreds of years, but their traditions were now being brought into question. They didn't like it at all. They began to plot how to have the Son suppressed, permanently. Surely, that was God's will. So, the Religion leaders used their power to manipulate the government to help them execute their plan. They were the ones behind the mob that was coming to take the Son.

The Religion leaders didn't believe who the Son claimed to be. He caused countless miracles and brought wondrous signs as proof of his identity and good intentions, but they didn't care. What they cared about was keeping rules, no matter who got trampled in the process. They claimed to speak for Elohim, but they didn't understand him at all. Their spirits' eyes and ears were closed.

These Religion leaders——the ones who knew the ancient written words of Elohim better than anyone else, who knew the prophecies, who should have known everything about who the Son was and why he came——were the very ones to turn their backs on him, and used their great influence to convince others to turn their backs too. The very ones who had the knowledge and position to help him and help the People, were the very ones to first betray the Son, and to cause his precious People to turn against their long-awaited Rescuer.

But that was only the beginning of sorrows. The Son was not just betrayed by the Religion leaders. When the intimidation of the descending authorities began to set in, his dearest friends and companions, out of fear, either sold him out, abandoned, or betrayed him as well.

The ones he should have been able to look to and rely upon, their true colors now exposed.

9

How quickly things had changed.

The Son was equal with God but now living fully as a man, entrapped by all the confinements that being one of the People brings. Despite this, he had lived a blameless life, and gave all that he had. But it wasn't enough. The People, blinded and hating the truth, believed the lies spread about him and turned him over to cruel hands.

After being accused over and over by distorted, conflicting witnesses, and being passed off by those in power repeatedly because no leader wanted anything to do with him, he knowingly signed his own death sentence through his admission of guilt——that he was indeed Elohim's Son, the Rescuer. His admission, he knew, was a capital offense.

It had begun. His freedom was now gone. He had willingly placed his welfare in the hands of the merciless and the unfeeling. Though he could have at any time, he knew there was no turning back now. He had fully committed himself to the People, for better or for worse.

Now, as a willing victim of the powers that be, he would experience mental, emotional and physical abuse. The Son was now about to experience ultimate trauma and intimately know real pain.

Amidst the encouragement of riveted spectators, the Son would be bound, whipped to the edge of death, his limbs impaled, and his body punctured. All this after being beaten with clubs and having

To the Slaughter

his beard ripped out of his face by those who would be laughing and making fun of him. He would become a joke, a laughingstock. The epitome of bullying and victimization.

He would be disfigured. He would be made an ugly and terrifying sight for all to see. A sight that would cause the People to recoil in repulsion and disgust. And, in this manner, he would shoulder it—a large, wooden cross. His very own personal, smothering reality.

Then, stealing the only thing that belonged to him, the Romans would tear all his clothes off, exposing him to anyone who cared to look. He would be treated as a despised, common criminal; exploited, humiliated, violated, and shamed.

The Captivating One, an abomination.

10

This had been the plan the Son and Elohim had agreed on from the beginning.

As the Son hung on that cross, that feared and hated symbol of tyranny, severity, oppression, and punishment, he hung there an innocent man—the picture of injustice.

He had experienced rejection before. Not only by the People in his hometown who had belittled him (believing he couldn't possibly be anyone special), but also by the People who watched and were intrigued by him. They heard his words of love and guidance, and saw his supernatural acts of service and compassion, and still they turned away.

But now, even the ones who once said they loved him now hated him. The ones who praised him just days ago, were the ones who called for this abominable sentence to be carried out. The most loyal had scattered trying to save their own skins, or changed their mind about him completely, not believing someone executed as a criminal was worthy of their confidence. Yes, even his best friends had deserted him in his time of greatest need, leaving him lonely, neglected, and abandoned. Wouldn't this, of all times, be the day to stick around?

But worst of all, and likely the most dreaded moment for the Son in all he endured, was the moment his own loving Father, Elohim, turned his back on him.

As he hung there, pulverized and mangled, his blood drained and resembling little more than pulp, the Son was taking upon himself all the cumulative wrongs, evil, ugliness, disease, and curses of the People...past, present, and future. Elohim, out of his fiery passion and jealousy for the People, had expended every last bit of his fury, rage, vengeance, wrath, and hatred of sin and separation on his very own perfect Son. The Son literally absorbed all the pain, misery, and Confusion that the People had adopted as their own. His Father, perfect and pure, had to turn away from it.

That, was truly, hell on earth.

The Son, perfect and blameless, died a disgraceful and violent death, as the worst of the worst, the lowest of the low. The only man who never had to die, willingly experienced the sting of death.

But there was still even more to be done.

After his death, he went down, down, down; down into the realm of black, suffocating hopelessness—into Hades itself.

He had lived a life of being beaten down, but justice was finally going to be served. The Son, through his brazen sacrifice, forever satisfied the punishment for the People's hostility, offenses and crimes against Elohim. Therefore, he could go down and take back from Hades the power the People had given it so long ago when they first wronged Elohim—and return that power back to them. The People had messed things up, but the Son had fixed it all unequivocally. Now Hades and Confusion could do nothing to harm the People, unless the People allowed it. Through beautiful reunion with their Creator, they would have the light, life, peace, freedom, and triumph they had yearned for for so long.

When his victory in Hades was completed, the Son still had to rely on the Spirit of his Father to get him back out. But in the coming out, he rose as The Conqueror, and led the way out of the enslaving, black pit of despair for all those who would follow him. In his life with the People, and in his death, he went as low as anyone could ever go, so that when he rose, he would raise any, who would choose to follow him, out of the darkness, and into The Light.

Emergence of a New Paradigm

Jesus' being fully God in no way subtracted from the fact that he was, in every way, a man.

The Immortal King came to us, a mortal. He subjected himself to the worst of the mortal experience. When he returned to Paradise, he was immortal once again——yet, different. From that point on, with that mortal experience forever fresh in his consciousness, he is beyond sympathetic towards our condition. He is hyper-vigilant in fighting our battles. Even at this very moment, he fervently defends our case, and represents our cause. He has paid a very high price for us to win.

If anyone understands, it's Jesus.

He experienced death with us...

So that we would have real life with him....

He became poor...

    So we would be rich.

He was rejected...

    So we would be accepted.

He hungered and thirst...

    So we would be filled.

He mourned...

    So we would be comforted.

He overcame temptation...

    So we would overcome too.

He was beaten...

    So we would have peace.

He was made ugly...

    So we would be made beautiful.

He was wounded...

    So we would be healed.

He was bound...

    So we would be free.

He experienced injustice...

    So we would receive justice.

He was debased...

    So we would be made glorious.

He was betrayed...

    So we would have loyalty.

He was shamed...

    So we would be esteemed.

He was condemned...

    So we would be liberated.

He was shown no mercy...

    So we would be shown mercy.

He had sorrow...

    So we would have joy.

He was alone...

    So we never have to be.

He was abandoned...

    So we would be adopted.

"So then, since we have a great High Priest [Representative and Defender] who has entered heaven, Jesus the Son of God, let us hold firmly to what we believe. This High Priest of ours understands our weaknesses, for he faced all of the same testings we do, yet he did not sin. So let us come boldly to the throne of our gracious God. There we will receive his mercy, and we will find grace to help us when we need it most."

Hebrews 4:14-16 NLT (brackets added)
The Bible

About the Author

Kelli grew up in a Christian family, steeped in a lifestyle it was assumed their faith demanded. A set of rules to follow, however, turned out to fall painfully short. She always felt like she was in the dark, on the outside of some great cosmic secret. Early in adulthood, she heeded a voice calling her to embrace and pursue the Truth for herself. That pursuit, ongoing, became the axis of real change.

Years later, Kelli has the desire and mandate to empower others with the truths she has learned and experienced by sharing profoundly fundamental principles in a way that is unfiltered, unforced, and obtainable; to paint color into worlds that may have been gray.

Kelli now resides with her husband, Vincent, and their two daughters, Berlin and Petra, in the area of Cincinnati, Ohio.

www.ingramcontent.com/pod-product-compliance
Lightning Source LLC
Chambersburg PA
CBHW042056040426
42447CB00003B/242